Swimming Pool Innovations

Duane Forte & Darlene Claire Preussner

Swimming Pool Innovations

Duane Forte & Darlene Claire Preussner

Schiffer Publishing Ltd

4880 Lower Valley Road • Atglen, PA • 19310

Designed by Danielle D. Farmer
Cover Design by Bruce M. Waters
Type set in Bauhaus/Wendy

ISBN: 978-0-7643-3915-8
Printed in China

Schiffer Books are available at special
discounts for bulk purchases for sales
promotions or premiums. Special editions,
including personalized covers, corporate
imprints, and excerpts can be created in
large quantities for special needs. For more
information contact the publisher:

Published by Schiffer Publishing Ltd.
4880 Lower Valley Road
Atglen, PA 19310
Phone: (610) 593-1777;
Fax: (610) 593-2002
E-mail: Info@schifferbooks.com

For the largest selection of fine reference
books on this and related subjects, please
visit our website at
www.schifferbooks.com
We are always looking for people to write
books on new and related subjects. If you
have an idea for a book, please contact us
at proposals@schifferbooks.com

This book may be purchased from
the publisher.
Include $5.00 for shipping.
Please try your bookstore first.
You may write for a free catalog.

In Europe, Schiffer books are distributed by
Bushwood Books
6 Marksbury Ave.
Kew Gardens
Surrey TW9 4JF England
Phone: 44 (0) 20 8392 8585;
Fax: 44 (0) 20 8392 9876
E-mail: info@bushwoodbooks.co.uk
Website: www.bushwoodbooks.co.uk

Other Schiffer Books By The Author:
Outdoor Spaces in the Southwest,
978-0-7643-3214-2, $39.99

New Ideas for Living Outdoors,
978-0-7643-3533-4, $24.99

The Sustainable Landscape,
978-0-7643-3452-2, $29.99

Other Schiffer Books on Related Subjects:
International Award Winning Pools, Spas,
& Water Environments II,
978-0-7643-3802-1

Garden Pools and Swimming Ponds: Design,
Construction, and Landscape,
978-0-7643-3636-2, $29.99

Contents

Introduction

This backyard setting is perfect for recreation and relaxation.

Swimming pools and spas are not a modern innovation. Since ancient times, man-made water enclosures, called baths, have existed all over the world for the sole purpose of communal cleansing. As time went on, these water vessels became the main attraction for social and family recreation, exercise, and relaxation; the same as residential swimming pools and spas are today.

Once regarded as a status symbol available only to the wealthy, private swimming pools have become more commonplace thanks to improved building materials and advances in construction techniques. This also opened

This poolscape complements the formal architecture of the home.

The dark interior finish magnifies the reflective properties of the water.

the door to swimming pool design. No longer just a rectangular hole in the ground surrounded by stark concrete, now pools are built in just about any shape and style imaginable—suited to even small backyards and budgets. With the addition of features such as vanishing edges, boulder waterfalls, and fountain bubblers, the swimming pool is transformed into a dramatic and beautiful focal point in the landscape.

Water is just a part of the overall picture, although it may very well be the most significant investment and prominent element. As an extension to the home, the pool area functions as an outdoor room complete with kitchen islands, dining tables, fireplaces, and comfortable furniture for family and friends to relax and converse well past sundown.

Although a well-planned and designed backyard environment significantly increases the property value, most homeowners are looking to save money on the operation and maintenance. More often than not, economical savings translate into environmental savings with equipment that uses less energy, conserves water and other resources, and reduces noise.

Deck jets arch water over the plantings and into the pool.

With a view of the golf course, this pool is a perfect place to keep cool.

A tropical paradise is possible in your own backyard.

A sunken kitchen serves swimmers reluctant to leave the refreshing water.

With all of the innovations in swimming pool design, outdoor features, and operational equipment, the one constant that will always remain is the excitement and enjoyment a poolscape brings to people of all ages from all walks of life. We associate pools and spas with fun, entertainment, leisure, and even romance. With pools we make memories surrounded by loved ones. It is these experiences of living the good life that we cherish and that make swimming pools and spas desirable now and for many future generations to come.

One of the main benefits to pool ownership is spending quality time with family and friends.

Design of the Times

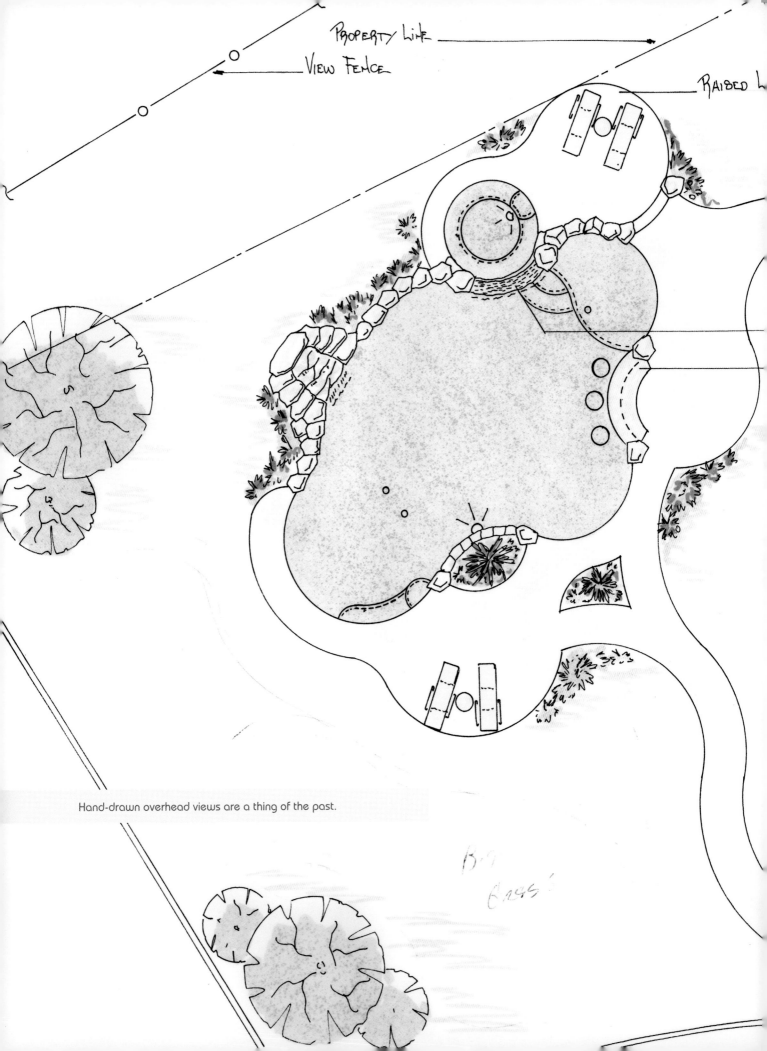

PROPERTY LINE

VIEW FENCE

RAISED L

Hand-drawn overhead views are a thing of the past.

AREA

EXISTING PATIO

LEDGER STONE SPILLWAY

TILED BAR TOP WITH 12 INCH OVERHANG

RESIDENCE

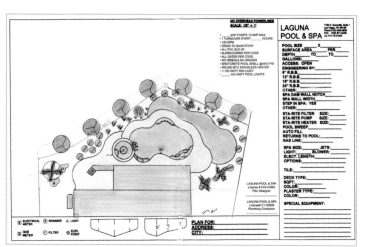

LAGUNA POOL & SPA

POOL SIZE _____ X _____
SURFACE AREA _____ PER _____
DEPTH _____ TO _____ TO _____
GALLONS: _____
ACCESS: OPEN _____
ENGINEERING BY: _____
6" R.B.B. _____
12" R.B.B. _____
18" R.B.B. _____
24" R.B.B. _____
OTHER: _____
SPA DAM WALL NOTCH _____
SPA WALL WIDTH _____
STEP IN SPA: YES _____
OTHER: _____

STA-RITE FILTER SIZE: _____
STA-RITE PUMP SIZE: _____
STA-RITE HEATER SIZE: _____
POOL SWEEP _____
AUTO FILL _____
RETURNS TO POOL: _____
GAS LINE: _____

SPA SIZE: _____ JETS: _____
LIGHT: _____ BLOWER: _____
ELECT. LENGTH: _____
OPTIONS: _____

TILE: _____

DECK TYPE: _____
SQFT: _____
COLOR: _____
PLASTER TYPE: _____
COLOR: _____

SPECIAL EQUIPMENT: _____

PLAN FOR: _____
ADDRESS: _____
CITY: _____

As with any construction project, building a swimming pool requires a cohesive plan. In the past, graphic presentations took long hours to complete utilizing the tools of the trade—pen, pencil, compass, and a drawing board. These simple renderings were a basic map of the property depicting the shape and size of the lot, the location of easements and setbacks, and the placement and configuration of the future swimming pool, spa, and landscape elements.

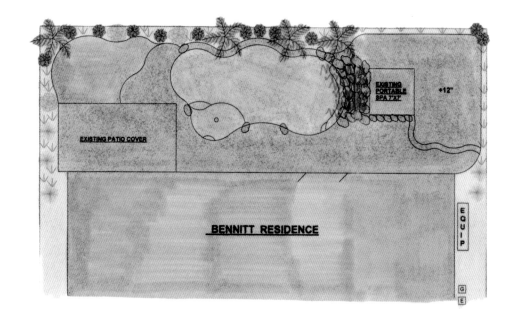

EXISTING PATIO COVER

EXISTING PORTABLE SPA 7'X7'

+12"

BENNITT RESIDENCE

EQUIP

FRONT COURTYARD

Hand-drawn renderings were time consuming to prepare.

Recently, the design process that has grown and gained the most attention is that which involves the computer. The development of CAD (computer aided design) systems began in the 1950s, but its widespread use for engineering applications took another 40 years. Today, CAD is used to generate two-dimensional scaled drawings used for the construction of a final design.

Diving boards and bright blue waterline tile are features from the past.

Stark concrete decking was standard practice many years ago.

Pool Studio® gives homeowners a virtual tour of their backyard design.

In 1999, Noah Nehlich, while completing a homework assignment, came to the realization that people love 3-D. At that time, 3-D modeling required working with difficult software programs. He developed Structure Studio so business professionals could create in 3-D. Pool Studio® is swimming pool design software for the pool industry that transforms flat two-dimensional designs into an interactive experience. Design presentations became a virtual tour of the property over life-like terrain full of vivid colors and natural textures, and complete with live action and sound. The program allows the viewer to examine the project from every angle and experience walking out a back door to see the sun shining through a rushing waterfall or the moonlight glistening off the still water of the pool on a starry night.

Pool design software allows for unique perspectives and overhead views.

Alterations and adjustments to the design are made in real time with the involvement of the homeowner. Multiple construction plans and layouts with detailed dimensions set to scale are produced from the final design and ready to build.

Swimming pools are no longer the plain rectangular or kidney shaped water holes surrounded by stark decking and set away from the house. Today's pools are designed to integrate seamlessly into the architectural style of the home and garden landscape. The swimming pool, adorned with such amenities as outdoor kitchens, fireplaces, swim up bars, grottos, and waterfalls is center stage for dining, relaxing, entertaining, or playing with family and friends.

ARTISTIC CONCEPTION

Pool Studio® allows features such as kitchens and fire pits to be integrated into the outdoor environment.

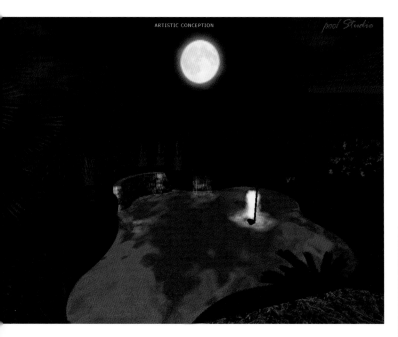

The design software gives the homeowner the opportunity to see the area at any time, day or night.

Technology has taken what was once only found in the creative imagination and made it possible. Pools and the elements that surround them are now seen as a separate architectural art form with myriad shapes, sizes, colors, materials, features, functionality, and beauty.

Shapes, Styles, & Pool Features

Not counting ancient pools, the history of residential swimming pools mostly began in Southern California, where about 20 pools a year were built in the early 1920s. A trend emerged in the mid 30s with newsreels and magazine photos of movie stars posing by their pools, and with the publicity of films like *Million Dollar Mermaid* starring Esther Williams. Pools became a desirable status symbol. They became even more popular with the post World War II housing boom and by 1947 there were 11,000 pools in the United States.

Aesthetically, pools were relatively limited. Most were either rectangular, oval, or kidney shaped with white plaster, blue waterline tile, bullnose coping, and occasionally a tile mosaic on the steps or bottom of the pool depicting fish or other ocean creatures. Positioned squarely in

the middle of the yard, dominating the landscape, or isolated away from the home, they became a completely separate destination, enjoyed only occasionally.

Today, all that has changed. Outdoor spaces now accommodate various functional as well as aesthetic considerations to contribute to the quality of life. They have become graceful extensions of the indoor living areas, creating a harmony between the home and the surrounding landscape.

Pools in the past lacked personality and style.

As an extension of the house, the pool area blends seamlessly with the architecture and landscape.

Water features, including swimming pools, are now fully integrated into these open air living rooms, drawing attention and visitors as they shimmer in the sunlight. Where water exists, it is noticed. Our eyes are drawn to water in a space before anything else—it serves the vital role of providing a focal point.

Welcomed by a large contemporary koi pond, visitors cross an artistic metal bridge to the matching front entrance of the home.

One of the most distinctive characteristics of today's outdoor living environments is the capacity for variety, and swimming pools and water accents are no exception.

Floating pads add interest to the geometric design.

Palm trees and thatched roofs complete he natural setting around the waterfall.

Centered within the pool, a fountain creates a stunning focal feature.

A grotto within the boulder waterfall is a favorite spot for children.

Waterfalls

Waterfalls come in a wide range of styles and with a variety of effects. Whether constructed of stones excavated from the site to resemble a natural setting, or hand crafted from man-made materials as an artistic design statement, all waterfalls have one thing in common—a change in level. How and where the water falls is dependent on the effect you wish to achieve. Spilling water over a smooth surface forms a sparkling uninterrupted ribbon. Place an obstacle in its path, and the ribbon is cut into sections. Water dropped a great distance makes a fine mist of tiny droplets that form rainbows when struck by sunlight. A large volume of water pouring over a high flat ledge creates a sheer curtain perfect for concealing a recessed grotto.

It is important that the waterfall is the appropriate size and scale for the property and complementary to the other elements of the overall landscape. Building a waterfall that is a harmonious blend of design and function requires some artistic and technical expertise. The end result adds beauty and drama to your outdoor retreat, while masking the intrusive noise of nearby traffic, neighbors, or an air conditioning unit.

A man-made boulder waterfall appears natural with surrounding landscape and plantings within the faux rocks.

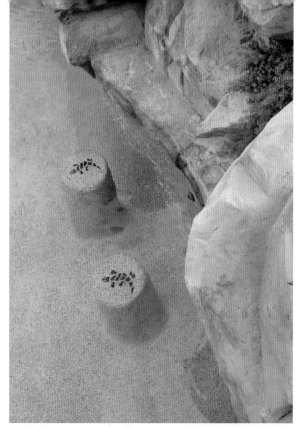

Underwater seats allow swimmers a place to rest and enjoy the sounds of falling water.

Built on the back side of the structure, this outdoor shower is screened from view.

Turquoise water gives this retreat a tropical feel.

A fountain bubbler shoots water from within the structure.

Planting native vegetation in and around the man-made boulders creates a more realistic appearance.

This backyard paradise could easily pass as a seaside resort.

Bubblers shoot up from the wet deck and balance the waterfall design.

Large boulders set in the concrete deck add seating options to enjoy the waterfall.

Water cascades down multiple levels before spilling into the pool.

The sound created from this triple waterfall masks the noise of nearby traffic.

A Tiki stands guard over this tropical paradise.

Even a small waterfall can add beauty and vertical interest to an area.

The waterfall creates an ideal privacy wall for those relaxing in the spa.

A variety of sounds, from trickling to splashing to gushing, can be created with waterfalls.

Water drops down to keep the slide wet and wild.

Slides

There are other ways to experience the thrill of slipping down a slope and plunging into the pool without the eyesore of a metal ladder and old-fashioned blue fiberglass chute. Incorporating a slide into your waterfall will increase the visual appeal and entertainment value for children and adults alike. Concealed within the structure or behind a curtain of water, recessed caves or grottos are wonderful places to explore and let your imagination run wild.

A functional feature can be incorporated without spoiling the aesthetics of the waterfall.

If sliding down a trough enclosed by hand crafted boulders and artificial rockwork doesn't suit your personality or taste, consider covering the fun feature with smooth colorful tile to create your own slip-sliding work of watery art.

Highly compacted soil and steel reinforcement are needed to prevent differential movement, which can cause cracks or even structural failure. Erecting a safe and stable water slide requires a well-planned design, careful engineering, and experienced pool building professionals as well as an increased depth in the pool where people shoot off the end of the slide.

Dual slides balance this poolside structure.

Tile resembling the pool color surfaces the slide.

The slide is surfaced to blend with the waterfall.

This handsomely tiled slide doubles as an artistic water feature.

Beach Entry

A beach entry, or zero entry, swimming pool has one end or entry that gradually slopes from the deck into the water in the manner of a natural beach. Finished with light brown or tan pebbles, or aggregate colored to look like sand, the beach entry is often used in lagoon style or tropical swimming pool designs.

Entering the pool gradually with each step and without stairs or ladders to navigate is a useful advantage for older people, young children, and those who experience problems with accessibility.

The gradual beach entry is decorated with mosaic tile to complete the tropical theme.

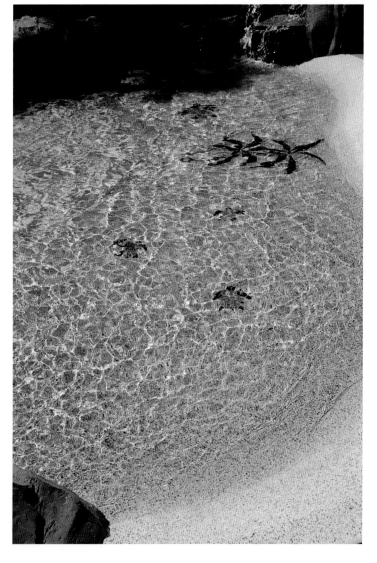

44

The light colored interior finish identifies the beach entry.

Here the wet deck is of a darker color.

Wet Decks

Most homeowners and their guests spend more time lounging in and around the pool than they do actually swimming. Wet decks are ideal for utilizing the pool area as a place to relax in the cool, soothing water. Multifunctional, the wet deck is basically an oversized step or landing area where several lounge chairs can be placed in the pool itself. Plastic or resin furniture is recommended since the pool chemicals will deteriorate and rust metal. Strategically installed umbrella sleeves provide a portal for removable shade and protection from the relentless desert sun. Incorporating a flat-topped boulder or other raised surface serves as a floating table for beverages or sunscreen.

The wet deck is perfect for placing lounge chairs within the pool itself.

To fulfill individual needs, wet decks can be designed at different levels. Installing the wet deck on the first step submerges it 6 inches below the waterline, perfect for all members of the family—children, seniors, physically handicapped, and pets—to splash and play or relax and enjoy the refreshing pool water. When positioned on the second step, the wet deck is 18 inches below the waterline and becomes more of an underwater bench. Using both levels in the design allows for more options and added pleasure.

Water arches over this expansive wet deck.

Tiling the wet deck makes for a smooth, non-slip surface.

The wet deck is basically an oversized first step.

The wet deck mirrors the shape
of the elevated spa.

Round, bright blue tile makes the wet deck
and seating ledge easily visible.

Infinity Edge

Water can link personal space with the surrounding environment. The best example of this is the infinity edge pool. Also known as negative edge, zero edge, or vanishing edge, it is a swimming or reflecting pool that creates a visual effect of water merging into the distant horizon or extending into infinity. In reality, the pool water spills into a hidden trough or catch basin where it is pumped back into the pool. The flat surface of the water draws the eye to the artificial horizon and the scene beyond takes on an increased significance. The distant view becomes part of the intimate foreground. The impact of the borrowed landscape is magnified in the mirror-like surface of the pool.

An additional water feature is created by the elegantly tiled catch basin of the infinity edge pool.

The flat surface of an infinity edge pool
creates mirror-like reflections.

Also called a negative edge pool, the water appears to fall off the edge of the property.

The scene beyond an infinity edge pool takes on an increased significance.

Also known as zero edge for the non-existent wall on one side, this type of pool creates an optical illusion.

An artificial boulder rests precariously on this negative edge.

Still, calm water is the result of an infinity edge pool.

Both the elevated spa and pool have the negative edge design.

Lap Pools & Swim Spas

Swimming is an excellent low-impact aerobic exercise. For homeowners who are health conscious and use water for fitness purposes, lap pools and swim spas are ideal options.

The lap pool blends seamlessly with the geometric design and architectural style of the home.

The dark interior finish attracts
the warmth of the sun.

Suitable to most lots, lap pools
are simple in design, being little
more than a long narrow lane for
swimming. A lap pool is generally 40
to 75 feet long, 8 to 10 feet wide and
at least 3 1/2 feet deep. The walls
at the end of the lane should be flat
and parallel to accommodate flip
turns. The steps are designed to
not interfere with swimming, and
often the ladder is recessed into
the sidewall with a handrail built
into the deck for support. Marking
the steps and swim lane with tile
adds a decorative element to
the pool while helping to keep
swimmers on course.

A compact alternative to the lap pool
is a swim spa, occupying less space
and using less water; they can
easily fit into the smallest of

Plant material protects this lap pool
from the wind and prying eyes.

backyards. Larger than most spas,
they average 13 to 20 feet long
and are equipped with adjustable
water jets that create a current to
swim against. Functioning much like
a treadmill for jogging, the swim
spa allows you to swim in place.
To increase the intensity of the
workout or accommodate different
strength and endurance abilities,
simply adjust the jets accordingly.
By installing massaging hydro-jets,
the swim spa can double as a spa
for therapeutic relaxation or romantic
stimulation. Be sure to allow enough
time for the water to heat up or cool
down between activities. The ideal
temperature is 78 to 82 degrees for
swimming and 96 to 104 degrees
for hydrotherapy.

The spa water spills into the lap pool to keep
it a comfortable temperature.

Commonly called spools, swim spas are a combination of both a pool and spa.

Identifiers known as target tiles clearly mark the seating bench of the spa.

Spas

For centuries we have immersed ourselves in warm water to relax our tense muscles and relieve our troubled minds. The ancient Romans erected spas (called baths) wherever they discovered natural hot springs. The therapeutic benefits are well substantiated. According to the Association of Pool and Spa Professionals (APSP), the typical spa at 104 degrees Fahrenheit not only relaxes muscles, but also dilates blood vessels, lowering blood pressure. The buoyancy of water counteracts gravity reducing the strain on muscles and joints and sitting submerged to your shoulders can make your heart 10-20% more efficient. And when you consider the hydro-jets that massages the neck, back, and feet, its no wonder why spas are one of the most popular of all water accessories.

This spa is encircled with the same man-made rock as a nearby waterfall.

Spilling from an elevated spa creates water music to be enjoyed in the pool area.

A custom-built spa can be any shape imaginable.

Square porcelain tile adorning the spa completes the geometric design.

This spa is capped to match the pool coping.

The ranch style home influenced the horseshoe shape of the spa.

Whether built simultaneously and connected to the swimming pool or as a separate entity, in-ground spas have limitless design possibilities. Styles can vary from minimalist designs that blend almost seamlessly with the decking to a naturalistic hot spring within a boulder waterfall and grotto to a highly stylized feature decorated with vibrant tile in interesting patterns. Ideally, the spa should complement the architecture of the home, the surrounding

outdoor environment, and the lifestyle of the homeowner.

When raised above the pool or elevated on the deck, the spa provides a perfect vantage point to enjoy the mirror-like reflections in the pool water or the activities of swimmers. This is ideal for adults who want to keep a watchful eye on children but stay removed from the splashing and screaming. As a standalone element tucked away in a corner or placed just off of a master bedroom, the spa makes an ideal secluded hideaway or romantic destination.

Spa spillways create another water element pleasing to the eye and ear.

The natural stone finish blends perfectly with the home.

The spill ledge of the spa drops a curtain of water into the pool.

This contemporary style repeats the geometric shape found throughout the yard.

Tucked away in a corner, this spa is an ideal secluded hideaway for relaxation.

Surrounded by water, a bridge allows access to the spa within a pool.

Water falls from several levels of an elevated spa.

The spa mirrors the design of the pool beyond.

Visitors to the spa can enjoy the culinary delights from the outdoor kitchen nearby.

Beautifully tiled columns spill water, mimicking the spa.

Mosaic tile accents the spa and attached fire table.

The light colored tile gives this spa a classic look.

Steam rises from the therapeutic circulating water.

A warming fire pit and seating area accommodates bathers exiting the water.

Natural stone faces and caps this oversized freeform spa.

Stacked stone creates this spa spillway.

A pre-manufactured, portable spa is customized with an elevated deck.

Different interior finishes create a contrast between the pool and spa.

Like a mini geyser, water shoots from a fountain bubbler in the pool wet deck.

Delightful sights and sounds are made with water in motion.

Water in motion is mesmerizing. Whether it bubbles up, spills over, or rains down, we are entranced. As it gushes, splashes, or trickles, the soothing sounds of aquatic music flood over our bodies and seep into our souls. Adding the vertical element of moving water allows the overall design to spring to life.

Multiple bubblers give this design a more formal appearance.

There is an infinite number of water features available to homeowners when you factor in size, shape, style, finish material, flow rate, acoustics, and even lighting and the astonishing effects that result.

Fountain bubblers shoot up from the pool floor, usually a wet deck or shallow ledge, like a mini geyser. They enhance almost any poolscape and are a favorite among children. A sheer descent is a sheet of water that flows down from a flattened

spillway while a rain descent creates individual thin streams of water more like a beaded curtain.

Scuppers are most often made of metal and direct the water over a small ledge before it falls into the pool. Sconces are decorative features mounted flush against a wall from which a stream of water spouts. Wok pots or spill pots are vessels, usually made of concrete, that sit outside the pool and spill water into it.

Deck jets shoot a narrow stream of air and water in an arc from the deck into the pool. Laminar jets produce a steady, bubble-free arc that appears more like a glass tube full of vibrant color with LED lighting.

A hotel pool becomes animated and playful with fountain bubblers.

Bubblers are usually adjustable for varying heights.

A sheer descent creates a sheet of water which pours into a pool aglow from a changing-color LED light fixture.

Fountains can be fixtures that rest on the edge and spill water into the pool fully incorporated into the plumbing system or totally self-contained with a basin and placed a distance away from the pool.

To achieve awe-inspiring results from the water feature you implement, keep in mind that it must compliment the other elements of the design and be appropriate in size and scale for the property.

Water pours from a scupper on a glass mosaic-tiled wall.

A sheer descent drops a curtain of water from the center of a beautifully detailed privacy wall.

Twin sheets of water fall from an elevated lounge area.

Sheer descents create soothing sounds and mask unwanted noise.

A rain descent drops thin streams of water that sparkle in the sunlight.

Water pours from multiple sheer descents, drawing attention to the colorful plantings.

The eye is drawn to the rain descent centered in the planter wall and then to the golf course beyond.

Water rains down from a ledge hosting a fire bowl, and from the balcony on the opposite side.

Aluminum scuppers deliver water to the pool and add interest to the angular design.

The rustic look of these scuppers match
the natural design.

Scuppers pour water from the backrest of a fire pit seating area.

Deck jets shoot a steady stream into the swim spa.

Concrete wok bowls are an attractive decorative element without pouring water.

Water gently pours from dual wok bowls.

The arching deck jet directs the eye to the sheer descent across the pool.

Water cascading down steps creates this focal feature.

Elegant lion fountains guard the formal landscape.

Water twists and turns its way down this unique fountain.

A simple three-tiered fountain adds water music to the environment.

A Buddha head fountain evokes peace and tranquility.

Features Around the Pool

Today's outdoor kitchens have all the amenities of their indoor counterparts, and more.

Outdoor Kitchens

The ancient Greeks believed that conversation and food had more flavor in the open air. This belief is evident today in the enormous appeal of outdoor kitchens. Modest "summer kitchens" have been around for many years. Built to keep the house cool, they were little more than a place to cook and eat. Recent outdoor kitchens and dining areas rival that of their indoor counterpart and match the home in quality, style, performance, and good looks.

At its most basic, an outdoor kitchen requires a place to cook, a place to set down food going on to and coming off the grill, and a place to sit and enjoy the incomparable flavor of food cooked in the open air. Locating the culinary area near an entry to the home, preferably by the indoor kitchen, allows for easy access to necessary supplies and makes cleaning up afterward more convenient. Another great advantage is existing utilities are close by, so running water, gas, and electricity is less expensive. Its location near or even attached to the house can also provide added protection from the elements.

Handsomely detailed, this complete culinary area overlooks the entire property.

Custom-built outdoor kitchens are designed and equipped to function most efficiently for the way the residents cook, how often they cook, and for how many and the type of food prepared. Adequate storage space and level surfaces for preparing and serving food are a must. Whether the outdoor kitchen is simple or elaborate, manufacturers offer a wide range of appliances that will suit every climate, lifestyle, and budget. Stainless steel seems to be the material of choice because it is rust resistant, easy to clean, and looks marvelous.

The grill is the heart of any outdoor kitchen and will serve its purpose for many years if you choose a model that is well made with heavy gauge metal. The joints should be welded and polished smooth. Make sure the handle is made from a material.

The grilling area of this sunken kitchen is well below the waterline.

that does not conduct heat and there is enough space between it and the grill hood for your hand to fit safely. The grates need to be sturdy and not too far apart and a thermometer should be placed where it is easy to see the temperature inside the closed grill.

There is a wide selection of outdoor equipment available to add convenience while cooking and entertaining outside. Under-counter refrigerators keep food and drinks cold and close at hand when the weather is warm. Complete ready-made refreshment centers often include a sink, condiment trays, and an ice bin; mounted on the front face is a rack for bottles, a bottle opener, and a towel holder.

Shaded by a palapa, the sunken kitchen is ready to serve swim-up guests.

Task lighting provides a high level of focused light on a work surface and can be recessed or surface mounted. Spotlights with flexible arms are made exclusively for outdoor cooking and are usually mounted on the countertop near the grill.

Cooking outdoors is a social event and creating a relaxed comfortable atmosphere is key. Provide plenty of shade on hot, sunny days or even consider installing an overhead fan in warmer climates. The fan can also help disperse the smoke coming off of the grill. A fire or heater can warm an area enough to take the chill

Large, removable umbrellas protect guests at the eating countertop from the elements, day or night.

off of the evening air. Seating should be conveniently located and adequately cushioned. Since guests always seem to congregate around the kitchen to converse with the chef, consider a bar-height counter for a seating and dining option. Bar stools come in a standard height of 25-26" for a 36" high counter. It is best to allow at least 10" between the top of the stool and the counter.

Make sure the materials used to construct and accessorize your outdoor kitchen are durable and weatherproof and your new cooking environment may be enjoyed more often than the one indoors.

This curved grilling station has a pass-through window to the indoor kitchen.

The countertop and backsplash tile resembles the pool water beyond.

Attaching the outdoor kitchen to the house provides easy access to utilities and added protection from the elements.

With the outdoor kitchen built flush against the home's exterior wall, the elegant patio can accommodate more guests.

Placing the cooking area at the far end keeps this rustic outdoor dining room free of smoke.

This U-shaped kitchen has plenty of counter space for food preparation.

This sunken kitchen has hidden storage areas for necessary supplies.

Refreshments await atop a
floating table.

Tikis support the thatched roof covering a tropical cooking area.

A free-standing structure elegantly protects the cooking and refreshment center.

A bar-height fire pit warms guests dining al fresco.

Matching natural stone adorns the fire pit and cooking center.

Bar stools await guests at an outdoor beverage center.

This U-shaped kitchen features a kegerator for cold beer on tap.

This simple grilling station is complete with an attached dining table.

Stainless steel is a durable, weatherproof material commonly used for outdoor amenities.

Comfortable seating creates a relaxed atmosphere for socializing.

A louvered cover allows for the ventilation of smoke.

Flagstone facing on this compact cooking station completes the naturalistic style.

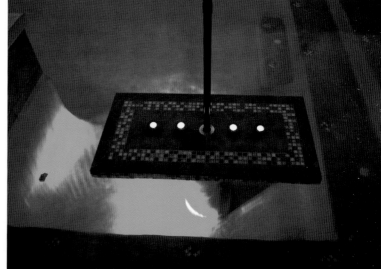

Floating tables accommodate swimmers not ready to leave the refreshing water.

This sunken kitchen hosts a spectacular view of the golf course below.

Granite makes for a durable and
attractive countertop material.

Situated between the spa and dining area, this fire table casts a warm glow over both.

Fire Pits & Fireplaces

Fire outside is alluring. The dancing flames, penetrating glow, and gentle roar awaken memories and instincts lying deep within our universal unconscious. The natural love and fear of fire is inherent in all of us. A recent discovery of fire-hardened clay in an African cave is evidence of the intentional use of fire dating back one to one and a half million years ago. For generations, domestic fire has held a prominent position as the focus for family life, the heart of social intimacy, radiating warmth for fundamental needs and inspiring myths and legends. Today, the quest for fire has taken the form of backyard bonfires and outdoor hearths in an urban jungle.

We have expanded our living space outdoors seeking ways to make our limited time at home more enjoyable and relaxing. Adding the element of fire opens up the dark of night, takes the bite out of the cold, and lengthens the outdoor living season. Fire outside is much more than a thing, it is an event. A backyard blaze encourages social interaction in a relaxed comfortable atmosphere.

A fire pit warms an elevated seating area.

Geometric patterns prevail in this quaint social setting.

Flames take away the chill when exiting the spa.

Cushioned chairs ensure socializing late into the night.

Identify the fire feature that will gratify your personal taste and architectural style and satisfy your primordial urge. At the very least, the fire feature will need to contain and control the blaze, reflect heat, offer views of the flames, and divert smoke away from the sitting area.

Fire pits are as close to a campfire as you will get within city limits, although most are fueled by natural gas. Whether they are just above ground level or tabletop or bar height and surrounded by tall stools, fire pits are the central feature in a sitting area and must be well ventilated. Gas fires put out a considerable amount of heat, as much as 60,000 to 75,000 BTUs (British Thermal Units) per hour, so keep seating at a safe distance. They can be built in a variety of shapes and sizes and finished with concrete, brick, stone, or tile and any combination of materials.

Fabricated logs made from recycled or reclaimed material is an environmentally sensitive alternative to burning wood.

A fireplace can turn up the heat on dramatic design and command a space like no other single feature. Yet it creates a warm, welcoming ambiance in any outdoor room. Fitted with removable grill irons, a spit, or a swinging kettle arm, fireplaces can be surprisingly versatile for cooking. Even when it is not lit, the fireplace can offer a warm focal point in an outdoor living environment.

Site your fire pit and/or freestanding fireplace at least 10 feet away from the house or other structures where there are no low-hanging branches overhead. Check with your local building department for regulations and restrictions that apply to your area.

This ground-level fire pit looks almost primordial.

The wide cap of the fire pit provides a place to set a plate of food or a drink.

This fire bowl contains the flames but allows for all-around viewing.

Built-in bench-style seating is ready for socializing.

Custom-built fire pits are as unique and imaginative as the homeowners.

This fire pit is located close to the spa to warm emerging bathers, yet visible throughout the entire property.

Situated on the pool's edge, the fire pit can double as a water feature.

Fire pits are a central feature in a seating area.

The circular fire pit mimics the spa on the other side of the bridge.

Blue fire glass, the color of the pool water, fills these fire boxes.

A bar-height fire pit warms diners seated at an outdoor kitchen.

A low-profile fire bowl sits atop a table vibrantly tiled in glass mosaic.

An angular fire pit with linear built-in seating is part of a contemporary design.

Combining fire and water creates a mesmerizing effect. The fire bowl appears to float on top of the water as it spills over the iridescent glass tile.

Seating for this fire pit is available above and below the waterline.

Flames dance above recycled fire glass within the feature.

The long fire table leads the eye towards the
infinity edge pool and the distant view.

Even when not aflame, an outdoor hearth is a warming focal point in the garden.

Handsomely finished, its not hard to imagine this fireplace indoors.

This rustic stone fireplace suits the natural setting.

This majestic fireplace commands center stage in an outdoor living room.

Extended built-in bench seating anchors the overhead patio cover.

This tall, stacked-stone fireplace features an inset mantle shelf.

Small or large, fireplaces graciously anchor an outdoor living area.

Equipment

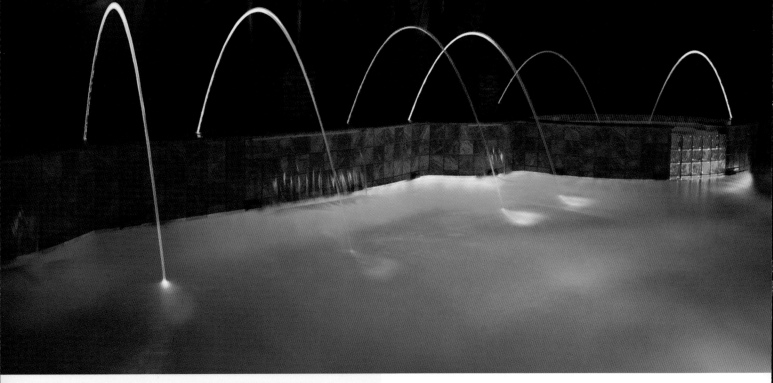

LEDs provide an ever-changing light and water display.

More important than ever before is the need for environmental responsibility. With a growing number of pool owners dedicated to being eco-friendly came the demand for products that are energy efficient, conserve water, and reduce noise. Using less electricity and water saves money as well as the environment.

The pool pump moves water through the components of the system, such as the filter, heater, water features, and plumbing and should circulate the entire volume of water at least once a day.

Vibrant colors in the laminar jets and the spa are achieved with LED lighting.

Lighting extends the time spent outdoors.

Older pumps are manufactured with a preset speed that cannot be adjusted. The faster you circulate or filter the pool, the more energy consumed.

Variable speed pumps are programmable, allowing for customized settings at the desired flow rate to perform each function, thereby using just the right amount of electricity necessary and no more. Running the pump at a slower speed for a longer period of time can save up to 80% on pool operating costs. Moving the water slower and with less pressure reduces friction, making it run cooler, quieter, and more efficient, which extends the life of the equipment.

High-efficiency light emitting diodes (LEDs) are in great demand because of the many benefits over common incandescent lighting systems. The greatest advantage is LED lights can save nearly 85% in energy consumption over other underwater lights. A 70 watt LED fixture produces approximately the same illumination as a 450 watt incandescent fixture. They generate up to 80% of light energy compared to just 20% of the incandescent bulb, which wastes the majority of its power on heat. LEDs produce very little heat, whether you leave your pool lights on for five minutes or five hours.

Extremely durable, LED lights last up to five times longer than traditional bulbs and are 100% maintenance free. The estimated life of an LED is 100,000 hours, or up to 11 years. Some even come with a 15-year warranty. Manufacturers of LED pool lights now offer fixtures that change colors to create a unique atmosphere and further enhance your outdoor enjoyment and relaxation.

Underwater LED lights make the entire pool glow.

Technology of today has made it easier
for the pool owner to save money,
energy, water, and the environment.

Lighting

As the sun goes down and a hot summer day gives way to a cool dark night, the stage is set for dramatic lighting. Although lighting serves practical purposes, such as safety and security, it can also create an inviting atmosphere and establish a mood for the evening festivities.

Subdued lighting doesn't spoil the mystery of the darkness.

Outdoor lighting allows for entertaining under a canopy of stars.

Well-positioned outdoor lighting can make a small area appear spacious or a large setting more intimate. It can emphasize interesting architectural and landscape features while concealing others less attractive.

The reflective properties of water magnify the effects of outdoor lighting whether they are delicate and delightful or bold and beautiful. Underwater fixtures illuminate the pool, creating a subaquatic fantasy that can be both magical and mysterious.

Light can relax, disorient, and stimulate and has a profound effect on any environment.

Lighting creates contrasting colors—the red hot rocks and the cool blue water.

A kaleidoscope of colors are possible with LEDs, either constantly changing or left on a particular favorite.

The spa water is more inviting when illuminated with submerged lights.

Lighting can make drastic color
contrasts with dramatic results.

Variable-speed pumps deliver the exact amount of water needed to perform different tasks.

Pumps

Traditional pool pumps can consume as much energy as all other home appliances combined. They are definitely the second greatest consumer of power in the summertime after air conditioning. The reason is that most residential pools are equipped with 1 or 2 horsepower pumps run by induction motors which function at a static speed, using more energy than necessary to perform each specific task.

Changing all the rules are the IntelliFlo® by Pentair and the IntelliPro® by Sta-Rite, the first programmable, variable-speed pumps in the industry. These pumps are manufactured with on-board intelligence and breakthrough motor technology and create a more environmentally responsible equipment system. The variable speed drive, which operates much the same as a dimmer switch with light intensity, is possible by using a permanent magnet synchronous motor rather than a conventional induction motor, delivering the exact amount of water needed to perform different tasks. The result is an energy savings of up to 90%, even compared to high-efficiency 1- and 2-horsepower pumps.

Electronically controlled by an onboard computer, these intelligent pumps can be programmed to manage multiple functions, finding the lowest possible requirements to accomplish each task. A built-in diagnostics system, constantly monitoring water flow and electrical current, is capable of making adjustments in seconds and is self correcting in cases of loss of prime, flow interruption, under and over voltage, and over-heating or freezing. The IntelliFlo and IntelliPro are the first pumps available with an integrated Safety Vacuum Release System (SVRS) to protect against entrapment. An internal controller can detect drain blockage and automatically shut off.

A built-in diagnostic system in the variable-speed pump is capable of detecting freezing conditions to protect the equipment.

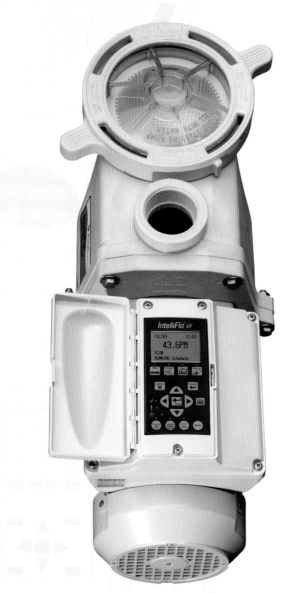

The permanent magnet motor in the variable speed pump produces less heat and vibration than a standard induction motor, resulting in substantial noise reduction, approximately 90%. The sound emitted is just 7 to 10 decibels, or about half as loud as a human whisper.

Since the variable speed pump works only as hard as it has to, the homeowner also benefits with its extended service life. The initial cost may be more than a conventional pump, but the money saved using a variable speed pump will more than pay for itself in no time at all.

The Intelliflo VS 3050 variable-speed pump by Pentair.

The Intelliflo VS 3050 opened to reveal the programmable panel.

The Intellipro VS 3050 variable-speed pump by Sta-Rite.

At the end of the nineteenth century, the first applications of electricity emerged in the factories to assist human workers with repetitive tasks. Automatic operation, or automation as it is now called, was born. Automated machines and technologies have taken over functions, systems, and processes once performed by people. Automation has become an integral part of our everyday lives.

Automation makes life easier for the pool owner by eliminating repeated trips to the equipment pad, memorizing operating sequences, opening and closing valves, and resetting time clocks and thermostats. Pentair, the global leader in pool and spa equipment, has developed a control system for every application, from simple to complex, along with the most advanced automation system in the industry, IntelliTouch®.

The system allows for one-touch centralized control over all pool and spa operations as well as additional poolscape features, such as lights, spa jets, waterfalls, and fountains. With the ability to operate up to 40 functions, total backyard automation is achievable.

The Intellitouch systems remote control.

With Intellitouch, total backyard automation is achievable.

The system involves just three key elements. The first is the enclosed power center located at the pool's equipment pad, which contains all of the electrical circuitry. Second is what Pentair refers to as a "personality kit," which determines the type and number of equipment and accessories controlled. The system controller is the final piece of the package and homeowners can select from an indoor wall-mounted control panel, Mobile Touch® wireless controller, Digital Tablet, In-Wall Touch Screen, Pocket PC, or standard PC interface.

All devices can also be mixed or matched. ScreenLogic® interfaces allow programming and operation of the system from devices that provide e-mail, web access, and other digital capabilities. For the ultimate in convenience, all key functions can be remotely controlled from across town or from halfway around the world.

To meet the growing consumer demand for home automation tools that are more capable and intuitive, all ScreenLogic systems can be upgraded to become an entire home

One-touch centralized control of all pool and spa operations is possible with the Intellitouch system.

The Intellitouch system load center.

automation system, including HVAC, lighting, home audio and video, irrigation, and much more.

Technically sophisticated, IntelliTouch features on-board diagnostics to verify correct operation of the pool equipment at peak efficiency for minimum energy usage. Capable of sensing conditions that could hamper operation, such as freezing, IntelliTouch automatically takes corrective action to protect the pool equipment. A diagnostic screen alerts the homeowner of the situation and reports when service is necessary.

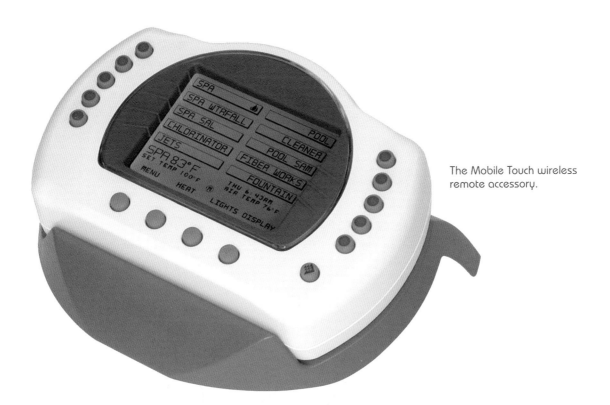

The Mobile Touch wireless remote accessory.

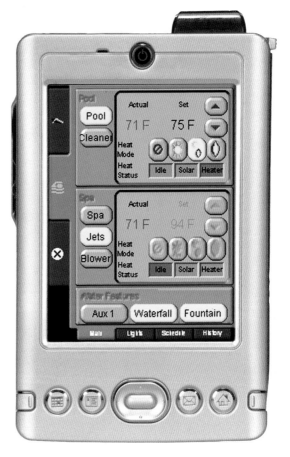

PDA color touch screen.

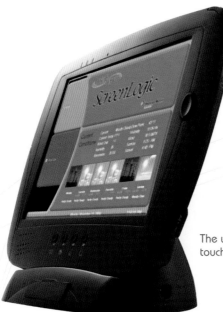

The wireless tablet color
touch screen.

The ScreenLogic app for iPhone
and iPod touch.

Intellitouch makes life simple and convenient for the pool owner.

Solar Heating

When you realize that just 20 days of sunshine produces the same amount of energy as all of the earth's reserves of oil, coal, and natural gas, it's difficult to ignore the awesome power of the sun. Determined to harness this clean, abundant energy source, Suntrek Industries was established in 1991 and has become a leading provider of solar electricity, hot water, and pool heating systems.

The solar collectors custom made from specially formulated EPDM elastomer cover approximately 80% of the surface area of the pool and are installed anywhere that receives direct sunlight. The roof is most often the best location. A temperature sensor on the roof sends a signal to the control system that the sun's energy can begin to heat your pool. A valve opens automatically and diverts the pool water to the solar heating collectors.

The solar collectors are custom made from specially formulated elastomer.

Most often mounted on the roof, solar collectors can be installed anywhere that receives direct sunlight.

The circulation pump pushes the water through the solar collectors and once the pool water has reached the desired temperature, the heating system will wait for the signal to heat your spa. This occurs automatically at the end of the filtration cycle and the collectors are isolated to the spa, bringing hot, therapeutic water to relax and sooth sore muscles.

The advantages of a solar pool heating system are many. No special maintenance is required under normal circumstances, although it is recommended that the system is turned off and drained in the winter if not in use. For a one-time-only installation charge, the pool water can be warmed 8 to 10 degrees above the pool's normal temperature, depending on weather patterns, without having to pay the heating utility costs, adding pollutants to the environment, nor depleting our natural resources. Finally, the life expectancy of the solar system is between 20 to 25 years.

Keeping It Clean

Clean, healthy water is an important aspect of pool ownership.

An in-floor cleaning system keeps the pool free of dirt and debris

Swimming pools and spas are meant for spending time with loved ones, having fun, and feeling relaxed. All pool owners desire clean, healthy water with a minimum amount of maintenance. Whether it is keeping it clear of debris or properly balancing the water chemistry, there is technology available today that allows pools to be virtually maintenance free.

In Floor Systems

Founded in 1964 to research, develop, and distribute pool and spa related products with an emphasis on automatic cleaning, Paramount Pool & Spa Systems has become one of the world's leading in-floor manufacturers.

The advent of in-floor cleaning and circulation systems can be attributed to the advancements in outdoor sprinkler technology. For many years, watering the lawn meant attaching an oscillating sprinkler head to the end of a hose and moving it by hand to different areas of the yard throughout the day. Today, automatic sprinkler systems do the work, driven by underground plumbing and hidden water valves.

Pool Tender®, an automatic cleaner for in-ground and above ground pools was released by Paramount in 1973.

The Paramount headquarters in Chandler, Arizona.

The research team at Paramount believed the same principle could be applied to swimming pools and first utilized a modified Toro® sprinkler head for in-floor installations. Paramount has developed state-of-the-art cleaning and circulation systems for concrete, vinyl, and fiberglass pools beginning with its first patent in 1967.

Each unique project is designed and engineered by a professional team at the company headquarters in Chandler, Arizona. The plans are sent to the pool contractor and the system is built right into the pool shell. It functions using rotating nozzles strategically placed in the floor, steps, and benches to sweep debris to the main drain and skimmer area. After about one hour, every square inch of the pool's interior will be swept one time, and after several hours is completely cleaned.

The pop-up rotating cleaning jets come with a lifetime limited warranty.

When the system is not operating, the nozzle retracts to be flush with the pool floor.

Another benefit of the in-floor cleaning system is improved water circulation. Whereas ordinary pools circulate water near the surface, the Paramount system evenly circulates the water throughout the pool. Independent studies have proven it creates cleaner, healthier, and more comfortable water while reducing the loss of chemicals and heat energy to the atmosphere.

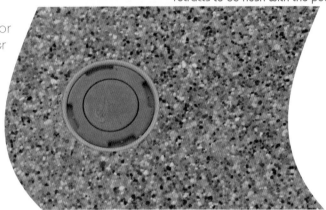

When the in-floor system is not operating, the nozzles retract flush with the pool floor, becoming virtually invisible. Built to last for the life of the pool, the company includes a lifetime warranty for replacement of all cleaning nozzles.

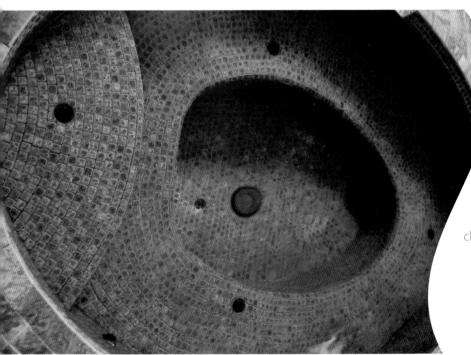

Nozzles are strategically placed in the floor, benches, and steps to sweep every inch of the pool and spa.

Water is circulated throughout the entire pool, reducing the loss of chemicals and heating energy.

Virtually maintenance free, an in-floor system gives the homeowner
more time to relax and enjoy the crystal clear water.

Ozone System

Paramount Pool & Spa Systems has been garnering attention since 2008 with the introduction of the Clear O_3® Ozone Purifying System.

Ozone is the cleanest, strongest non-chlorine shock available, oxygen being the only by-product it produces. Ozone breaks down any non-living waste product that can combine with chlorine causing irritation to the skin and eyes. These unhealthy particulates have also been linked to asthma and other ailments. Free from the unwanted particles, the chlorine is allowed to work more effectively as a disinfectant, reducing the demand for chemicals by up to 70%.

The Clear O_3 ozone system delivers ozone into the pool water using a suction injection system.

An ozone system breaks down unwanted pool particulates that irritate the eyes and skin.

Housed in an aluminum main body, ozone is created using an ultra-violet bulb specifically designed to excite ozone molecules extracted from the oxygen in the air. A suction injection system then mixes the ozone-enriched air with the water going into the pool.

Once a clean and clear swimming environment is achieved, the ozone reverts back to oxygen making it an eco-friendly purification process.

Salt Chlorination

All pool owners prefer equipment that minimizes time spent on maintenance and maximizes enjoyment in the water. Automatic chlorine generators also referred to as salt chlorinators, use ordinary table salt to produce all the chlorine your pool will ever need. This eliminates the purchase, transportation, storage, and handling of the harsh chemical.

The devices are plumbed in-line and use less than a teaspoon of table salt, or sodium chloride, added directly to the pool water prior to start up. Once dissolved, the salt flows over specially coated titanium electrode plates and is electrolytically converted into pure chlorine then distributed throughout the pool, sanitizing the water. Because the chlorine produced by the generator is pure, it eliminates the odor, stinging eyes, and irritated skin caused by the additives in packaged chlorine.

The Intellichlor® salt chlorinator is plumbed in-line and converts ordinary table salt into pure chlorine.

Electrolytic chlorine generation is the easiest, most effective, and convenient way to keep pool water clean.

Additional salt is needed only occasionally to replace what is lost due to splash out, backwashing, or pump out since the salt is recycled continuously through the circulation system.

Built into the salt cell is a controller that regulates chlorine production and a digital display for salt level, cell cleanliness, sanitizer output, and water flow. This makes the performance data easy to monitor. The new salt systems are self-cleaning and monitoring, equipped with an automatic reverse cycling feature to prevent salt build up and an automatic shut off to protect the unit from damage under low water temperature conditions.

A salt chlorinator sanitizes the pool water, keeping it fresh, clear, and safe.

Resources

The Association of Pool & Spa Professionals
2111 Eisenhower Avenue
Alexandria, VA 22314
(703) 838-0083
www.APSP.org

Pool & Spa News
6222 Wilshire Boulevard, Suite 600
Los Angeles, CA 90048
(323) 801-4972
www.poolspanews.com

AQUA
4130 Lien Road
Madison, WI 53704
(608) 249-0186
www.aquamagazine.com

Watershapes
6119 Lockhurst Drive
Woodland Hills, CA 91367
(714) 313-6136
www.watershapes.com

Pentair Water Pool & Spa, Pentair Pool Products, Sta-Rite
1620 Hawkins Avenue
Sanford, NC 27330
(800) 831-7133
www.pentairpool.com
www.staritepool.com

Paramount Pool & Spa Systems
295 East Corporate Place,
Suite 100
Chandler, AZ 85225
(800) 621-5886
www.1paramount.com

Structure Studios
3300 St. Rose Parkway, Suite 310
Henderson, NV 89052
(800) 778-8996
www.structurestudios.com

Suntrek
5 Holland, Building 215
Irvine CA 92618
(800) 292-7648
www.suntreksolar.com